This edition published in 1998 by
Broadman & Holman Publishers

ISBN 0-8054-1880-6

Text and illustrations copyright © 1998 Alicia Garcia de Lynam
This edition copyright © 1998 Lion Publishing

First edition 1998
10 9 8 7 6 5 4 3 2 1 0

Printed and bound in Italy

When the
World Was New

For Alex and mamá

When the World Was New

Alicia Garcia de Lynam

B&H
BROADMAN
& HOLMAN
PUBLISHERS

Have you ever wondered
what it was like
when the world was new?

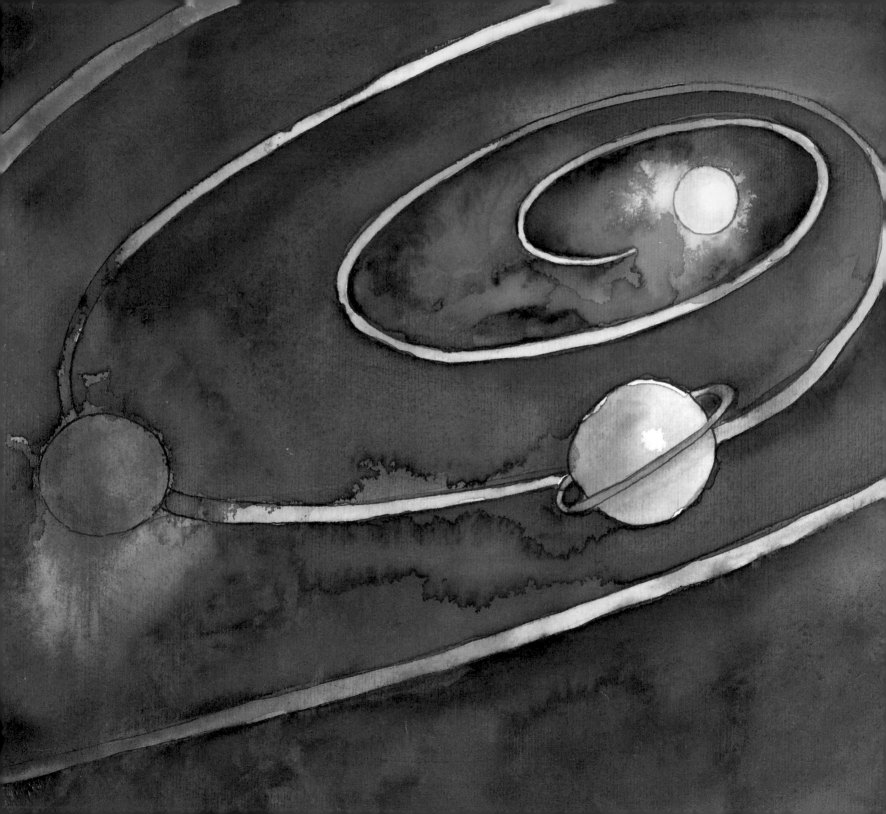

When the world was new,
what would have happened if
God had not made the sun,
moon, and stars?

There would still be nothing.

When the world was new,
what would have happened if
God had not turned on the lights?

It would be dark.

When the world was new,
what would have happened if
God had not pushed "start"?

There would be no seasons.

When the world was new,
what would have happened if
God had not turned off the rain?

There would be no land.

When the world was new,
what would have happened if
God had not made the plants?

There would be nothing
to eat or to enjoy.

When the world was new,
what would have happened if
God had not made the animals?

There would be no pets to cuddle,
or warm woolly sweaters.

When the world was new,
what would have happened if
God had not made us?

There would be no one to marvel
at the wonders of the world.

Isn't it great that God
made our world just right...

And then found time to have a rest!